Tom the Whistling Wonder

Story by Leon Rosselson
Pictures by John Haslam

OXFORD
UNIVERSITY PRESS

Danny, Melody and Rashid were mates. Danny was the leader or 'number one' because he was the biggest and he had the football.

When Danny had a cough and had to stay home, Melody was number one because she was Danny's cousin and she had the kite. When both Danny and Melody had coughs and had to stay home, Rashid became number one because he had the sailing boat and he was the only one left.

Then there was Tom. He trotted into the field where the three mates were deciding what to do on the first day of their summer holidays.

"I spy a stranger," Danny said.

"Can I play?" asked Tom.

"No way." Rashid shook his head. "We're mates."

"Can't I be one of your mates?" Tom asked.

"You're too small," Melody replied.

"I've been ill, but I'm better now so I expect I'll be growing soon."

"What have you got then?" Danny demanded.
Tom looked puzzled.

"I've brought a football, Melody's brought a kite
and Rashid's brought a sailing boat," Danny
explained. "What have you brought?"
Tom turned out his pockets. "Nothing."

"Nothing's no use," Rashid said.

"I've got a whistle," Tom said.
"Show us,"
"It's in my mouth,"
"Show us," demanded Danny.
"OK."
Then Tom looked up at the blue sky and began to whistle.

6

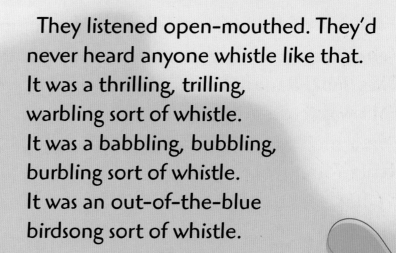

They listened open-mouthed. They'd never heard anyone whistle like that. It was a thrilling, trilling, warbling sort of whistle. It was a babbling, bubbling, burbling sort of whistle. It was an out-of-the-blue birdsong sort of whistle.

"That's a neat whistle," Melody said admiringly. "What do you all think?"

"Yes," said Rashid. "If he's a mate then I can tell him what to do."

"Suits me," agreed Danny. "OK. You can be number four, Tom."

"What does that mean?" asked Tom.

"It means," explained Rashid, "you have to do everything we tell you."

"But when we've all got coughs and have to stay home," added Melody, "you can be number one."

"Great!" exclaimed Tom. "Thanks."

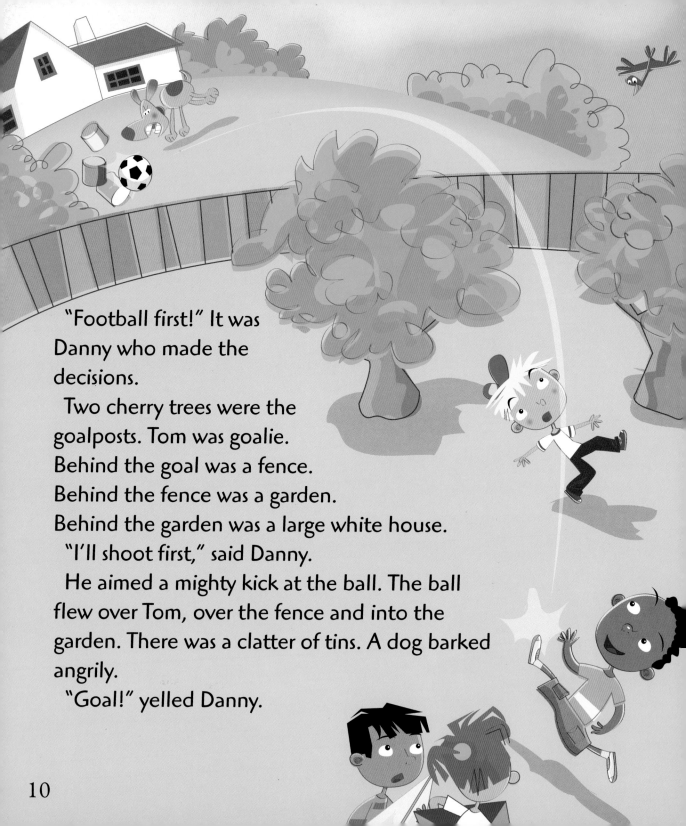

"Football first!" It was
Danny who made the
decisions.

Two cherry trees were the
goalposts. Tom was goalie.
Behind the goal was a fence.
Behind the fence was a garden.
Behind the garden was a large white house.

"I'll shoot first," said Danny.

He aimed a mighty kick at the ball. The ball
flew over Tom, over the fence and into the
garden. There was a clatter of tins. A dog barked
angrily.

"Goal!" yelled Danny.

They ran to the fence. It was too high to see over. Helped by Tom, Rashid and Melody, Danny tried to climb up the fence. There was a fierce growl and a furious burst of barking. A heavy shape threw itself against the other side of the fence. Danny fell backwards, knocking against Melody who fell against Rashid who fell against Tom who fell flat on his face.

"Wowee!" exclaimed Danny. "That's the monster dog from outer space."

11

"What now?" asked Melody.

"Now," ordered Danny, "you run round to the front door and ask for our ball back."

"Rashid," said Melody, "run round to the front door and ask for our ball back."

"Tom," said Rashid "run..."

"Do I have to?" asked Tom.

"You're number four mate," said Danny.

Tom sighed. Then pulling himself up to his full height and shaking the worry out of his head, he ran along and through and round and up to the front door of the large, white house.

Feeling small and rather anxious, he reached up to ring the bell. Then he crouched down on his marks ready to race away in case a monster from outer space came to the front door. But nobody came. Nobody at all. Tom skipped back to tell his mates the bad news.

"We'll get it later," said Danny. "Let's fly the kite."

They ran to the top of the hill. Rashid and Melody held the kite while Danny and Tom held the string. Rashid and Melody ran down the hill and then let go of the kite. Danny and Tom pulled on the string. The purple kite zoomed skywards. It zipped and zigged and zagged through the air like a wild bird trying to escape.

"Genius!" exclaimed Tom excitedly.

Zap! The kite crashed into the top of a chestnut tree and stayed there. Four sad faces looked up at it.

"What now?" asked Melody.

"Now," said Danny, "you climb the tree and bring it down."

"Rashid," said Melody, "climb the tree and bring it down."

"Tom...," said Rashid.

But Tom was already at the tree trying to scramble up it. It was hopeless. They all tried, helping each other up, climbing on each other's shoulders. It was no use. They couldn't even reach the first branch.

"We'll get it later," said Danny. "Let's sail the boat."

15

They ran to the pond. Rashid pushed the boat out. They raced round to catch it on the other side. The wind caught the sails. The boat curved gracefully along.

"Super!" exclaimed Tom admiringly.

Suddenly the wind dropped. The boat stopped curving gracefully along. Four sad faces stared at it drifting slowly round and round in the middle of the pond.

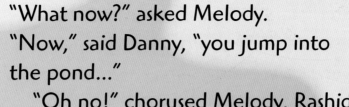

"What now?" asked Melody.
"Now," said Danny, "you jump into the pond..."

"Oh no!" chorused Melody, Rashid and Tom.

They sat on the edge of the pond wondering what to do.

"We've nothing to play with now," said Danny.

"My whistle," said Tom.
"What's the use of your whistle?" Rashid said.
"You never know," said Tom.

Tom looked up at the pale blue sky, took a deep
breath and whistled, a thrilling, trilling warbling sort
of whistle. A swallow swooped low over the
water. Then another. Then another. They
swept down so that their wings touched
the top of the sailing boat's mast. The
boat began to move. The boat began to
bob along, a gentle wind from the
swallows' wings filling its sails. Soon
Rashid reached out and rescued the
boat from the pond.

"Magic, Tom," Rashid said.

"The kite," Melody said. "Can you magic the kite, Tom?"

They stood round the tree. The kite was still tangled up in its branches. Tom took a deep breath and whistled again, a babbling, bubbling, burbling sort of whistle. They watched and waited. What were they waiting for?

A crow landed on the branches. It pecked at the kite. It took the kite in its beak and pulled. It pulled the kite free. The crow flew off, the kite still in its beak. Tom's whistle rose into the sky.

"Caw, caw," went the crow.

The kite dropped down into Melody's grateful hands.

"Magic, Tom," Melody said.

"Now for my football," Danny said.

They rolled a large rock up to the garden fence.
Danny and Melody climbed on it and peered
over. There was the ball, right near the fence.

"What about the monster dog?" Tom asked.
"Asleep," Danny said. "If we lift you over the
fence, you can grab the ball and then we'll pull
you back again."
"Help!" said Tom.
They pushed him up and lifted him over the fence.
The dog jumped up and growled angrily. Tom froze.

"Whistle, Tom, whistle," urged Melody. Tom whistled, an out-of-the-blue birdsong sort of whistle. The dog looked at him, stopped growling and wagged its tail. Tom grabbed the ball and threw it over the fence. Then he raised his arms so that Danny and Melody could pull him back over. You should have heard the cheers.

"You're a whizz at whistling," Rashid said.

"You're a wizard whistler," Melody added.

"You're a whistling wonder," Danny declared.

"Can I be number one then?" asked Tom.

"Well," said Danny, "what I think is – we can all be number one."

"Fantabulous!" exclaimed Tom happily.